Contents

EVERYTHING YOU NEED TO KNOW ABOUT YOUR IRA

In 5 Easy Steps

Sourced from Ed Slott and Company, LLC

Courtesy of Michael Reese
CFP®, CLU, ChFC, CTS

Created by Centennial Wealth Advisory, LLC and Centennial Advisors
with information provided by
© 2016 by IRAHelp, LLC

ISBN 978-1-365-46809-4

$23.7 Trillion.

According to the Employee Benefit Research Institute*, $23.7 Trillion is the amount of money that Americans have saved in qualified retirement plans. These include IRA, 401k, 403b, and all the rest of the related tax-qualified retirement plans.

Many Americans use these plans to save for their retirement, and perhaps you do as well. And why wouldn't you?

During your working years, these types of plans represent a terrific way to save for your future. You receive a tax deduction (typically) when you invest, your money grows tax-deferred, and you can often set it up to automatically draft deposits straight from your paycheck.

However, you also need to understand that these accounts come with strings attached. And if you pull the wrong string, you can end up unintentionally owing thousands of dollars to the IRS in unexpected taxes and penalties.

DON'T make that mistake!

I have put this booklet together utilizing the terrific resources available from Ed Slott and his Master Elite Advisor program to help you make good decisions with your retirement plans.

If you have any questions, you can always give me a call. We are here to help.

Enjoy,

Michael Reese, CFP®, CLU, ChFC, CTS

Founder

Centennial Wealth Advisory, LLC and Centennial Advisors

NORTHERN MICHIGAN

877.995.9575 | info@cen-wealth.com | Cen-Wealth.com

CENTRAL TEXAS

512.265.5000 | info@centennialadvisorstx.com | CentennialAdvisorsTX.com

https://www.ebri.org/publications/benfaq/index.cfm?fa=retfaq4

Choosing the Right Financial Advisor

Why do you need a financial advisor?
Today's financial landscape is as complicated as ever. A good financial advisor can help you navigate this complexity so that you can make educated, informed decisions on what is best for you and your family.

1. LOOK FOR A CERTIFIED FINANCIAL PLANNER™. Although many professionals may call themselves "financial planners," CFP® professionals have completed extensive training and experience requirements and are held to rigorous ethical standards. They understand all the complexities of the changing financial climate and will make recommendations in your best interest.

2. BEWARE REFERENCES. In today's financial world that has a hyper-sensitive focus on privacy, regulators have often taken the position that offering client references violates their privacy. Nowadays, when a financial advisor offers to share client references, then you know that they do not take privacy seriously. This is an advisor to avoid.

3. FIND A SPECIALIST. The term "Financial Advisor" is highly generic and can be used to describe many different types of professionals in the financial services field. When shopping around, find an advisor who specializes in your area of concern. If you had a heart problem, would you rather see your family doctor or a cardiologist? The same principle should apply to your financial advisor.

4. **ASK ABOUT EDUCATION/TRAINING.** Most financial advisors routinely participate in what are called "advanced training" classes. Many times these classes are heavy on sales training and light on "real" education. If you really want to know what your advisor has studied, ask to see the manual from the last educational conference he or she attended. If it has more sales information than technical information... Beware!

5. **DON'T BE AFRAID TO GET A SECOND OPINION.** Your IRA, 401(k) or other retirement account may be the largest single asset you own. If you're not sure about the advice you've been given, don't be afraid to get a second opinion. If an advisor tells you that there's no need for one, they're probably not confident in the information and recommendations they provided to you in the first place.

CHOOSING THE RIGHT TAX PROFESSIONAL

Why do you need a tax professional?
Managing taxes during retirement will be the single most important factor in determining your ultimate lifestyle. In addition to a financial planner and estate planning attorney, a qualified tax professional is an integral part of any planning team.

1. **ASK FOR REFERENCES.** Have you ever stopped to think about how you picked your doctor or mechanic? Chances are you chose them because a friend or family member recommended them based upon a positive experience. The same should be true of your tax professional. Often times, people are afraid to ask for advice from those closest to them when finances are involved, but picking the right tax professional is too big of a decision, so "do your homework" and ask around.

2. **CHECK FOR CREDENTIALS.** Not all tax preparers are CPAs. In fact, in many states, anyone can prepare tax returns and call themselves a tax professional. Most serious tax professionals will either be a CPA or an EA (Enrolled Agent). However, this does not necessarily mean that they are competent enough in the retirement area to assist you.

3. **ASK ABOUT EXPERIENCE.** In most cases, you would opt for experience over a novice. Do you really think your choice of a tax professional is that different? Sometimes, there is no substitute for experience. Ask your tax professional about cases similar to your own, how often they deal with them and how they typically handle them.

4. **ASK ABOUT EDUCATION/TRAINING.** When most people think "CPA," they think tax expert. But, the rules governing retirement accounts are highly complex and are constantly changing. If your tax professional is serious about this area of retirement planning, they will make sure to stay up-to-date on the latest tax law changes. Make sure to ask about the last conference or continuing education class they have attended on retirement planning.

5. **ASK ABOUT CONTINUITY.** Planning to maximize your retirement distributions and transfer your wealth is not a one-time deal. Some of your most important decisions may not be made for years, or even decades. If you don't expect your tax professional to still be working, you may want to ask what type of plan they have in place to make sure you will still receive the high level of advice you deserve when you need it the most.

CALCULATING YOUR RMD

What is an RMD (required minimum distribution)?
An RMD is the minimum amount that must be withdrawn from a retirement account each year.

When are you subject to RMDs?
Traditional IRA owners are subject to RMDs beginning in the year in which they turn age 70. Beneficiaries of IRAs and/or Roth IRAs are subject to RMDs beginning in the year after the year of the IRA (or Roth IRA) account owner's death.

1. **DETERMINE YOUR DISTRIBUTION YEAR.** The distribution year is the year for which you are taking a distribution, not necessarily the year in which you take that distribution. For instance, if you turn age 70 . in 2016, you do not have to take your first RMD until April 1, 2017. If you wait until April 1, 2017 to take that distribution however, the distribution year is still for 2016. In addition, you will have to take a second distribution by the end of 2017 for 2017. After the year you turn age 70 ., all distributions should be made by December 31 of each year for which they are being taken.

2. **FIND THE RETIREMENT PLAN BALANCE.** Use the balance as of December 31 of the prior year. Add back any outstanding rollovers and re-characterizations.

3. **DETERMINE THE LIFE EXPECTANCY FACTOR.** Most IRA owners look up their age on the Uniform Lifetime Table in order to determine their factor. If a spouse is the sole beneficiary of an IRA account for the entire year and is more than 10 years younger than the account owner, the Joint Life Expectancy Table is used. Most beneficiaries look up their life

expectancy in the year after the year of the account owner's death using the Single Life Table. Going forward each year that factor would simply be reduced by one (there are some exceptions for spousal beneficiaries). Make sure to look up the actual ages of the individual as of the last day of the year.

4. **MORE MATHEMATICS.** Divide the retirement plan balance (step 2) by the life expectancy factor (step 3). The result is the RMD that must be taken. Be sure to take the RMD by December 31 of the distribution year (except IRA owners in the year they turn 70 .). REMEMBER there is a 50% penalty for any portion of an RMD that is not taken.

5. **TAKE NOTICE.** RMDs from owned IRA accounts can be aggregated and RMDs from owned 403(b) accounts can be aggregated. Accounts inherited from the same person can aggregate RMDs. All other types of accounts cannot be aggregated.

Avoiding the 10% Penalty

What is the 10% penalty?

A 10% early distribution penalty applies to taxable distributions made before age 59 . Distributions made after age 59 . are not subject to the 10% early distribution penalty.

Exceptions apply for withdrawals from company retirement plans for individuals who separate from service at age 55 or older, and for withdrawals from governmental defined contribution and defined benefit plans for public safety officials who separate from service at age 50 or older. For SIMPLE IRAs, the penalty is 25% for the first two years in the plan, then reverts back to the 10% penalty in following years.

1. **CHECK THE AGE OF THE IRA OWNER, LOOK FOR AN EXCEPTION TO THE PENALTY.** The main exceptions are disability, death (distributions to beneficiaries are never subject to the penalty), medical expenses generally in excess of 7.5% to 10% of AGI (adjusted gross income) in the year of distribution, first-time home buyers, higher education expenses, an IRS levy and health insurance for the unemployed receiving unemployment compensation for 12 consecutive weeks.

2. **MAKE SURE THE EXCEPTION YOU WANT TO USE APPLIES TO THE TYPE OF PLAN YOU HAVE.** There are three categories of exceptions to the 10% early distribution penalty. Some exceptions apply to both IRAs and employer plans, some apply to IRAs only, and some apply to employer plans only. Be sure you use the right exception for your type of retirement account.

3. **THE EXPENSE MUST BE IN THE SAME YEAR AS THE IRA DISTRIBUTION.** For exceptions such as the higher education expense and the medical expense, make sure the IRA distribution is made in the same year the expense is incurred.

4. **SOME EXCEPTIONS APPLY WHEN THE DISTRIBUTION IS USED FOR A FAMILY MEMBER.** Exceptions such as death and disability only apply to the account owner. Other exceptions apply to family members such as spouses, children or grandchildren. Check with your financial advisor to find out the requirements of any exception for which you think you might qualify.

5. **HOW TO CLAIM AN EXCEPTION.** Many times the IRA custodian or plan administrator will issue the 1099-R for the distribution with a code saying that the distribution is early and no known exception applies. Don't give up. You should file IRS Form 5329 with your tax return to tell IRS what exception you are claiming.

FIXING A MISSED RMD

What is a missed RMD (required minimum distribution)?
RMDs must be taken by IRA owners beginning in the year they turn age 70 . and by IRA and non-spouse Roth beneficiaries beginning in the year after the death of the account owner. RMDs not taken are subject to a penalty of 50% of the amount not taken each year.

When should you look for a missed RMD?
You should look for a missed RMD every year after an account owner turns age 70 and when an IRA or non-spouse Roth beneficiary inherits an IRA. Ask your advisor to double check any calculations to be sure they are correct.

1. **LOOK AT THE BALANCE SHEET.** Determine the prior year-end IRA balance for the year that an RMD was not fully satisfied. (Note: There were no IRA RMDs for 2009.)

2. **DETERMINE THE LIFE EXPECTANCY FACTOR FOR ALL MISSED YEARS.** IRA owners use their age each year and look up the corresponding factor on the Uniform Lifetime Table. Non-spouse IRA beneficiaries use their age only in the year after the account owner's death and look up the corresponding factor on the Single Life Expectancy Table. In each subsequent year, a beneficiary will subtract one from the previous year's factor. (Remember: These are the general rules for determining life expectancy factors. There are many exceptions to these rules.)

3. **DO SOME SIMPLE MATH.** Divide the account balance by the life expectancy factor for each missed year's RMD and withdraw that amount from the IRA.

4. **IMPORTANT FORMS TO FILE.** File IRS Form 5329 for each missed RMD to report the missed distribution and penalty. The penalty can be waived for good cause. Attach a letter to the form requesting a waiver. It is helpful to include language in your letter explaining to the IRS why the distributions were missed, that the problem has been corrected and that procedures are in place to avoid future problems.

5. **IT WILL NEVER HAPPEN AGAIN.** Set up procedures to ensure you take future RMDs. Many custodians offer an option to distribute RMDs automatically each year. If you struggle to remember to take your RMD, setting up an automatic distribution may be beneficial.

Avoiding 60-Day Rollover Mistakes

What is a 60-day rollover?

A 60-day rollover is the distribution of funds from a qualifying retirement account payable to the account owner who then has 60 days to redeposit the funds into another qualifying retirement account.

1. **DO TRUSTEE-TO-TRUSTEE TRANSFERS INSTEAD.** The best way to avoid making a 60-day rollover mistake is to avoid 60-day rollovers! Transfer your funds directly to another retirement account. Not only does a direct transfer avoid any 60-day time problems, but if the rollover is coming from a 401(k) or other qualified plan, it will also avoid the mandatory 20% withholding requirement.

2. **MAKE CHECKS PAYABLE TO NEW IRA CUSTODIANS.** Sometimes the only way a custodian will distribute an IRA or other retirement account money is in the form of a check. There is a special rule that allows a distribution by check to qualify as a direct rollover (and avoid the 60-day rules) when the check is made payable to the new IRA. For example, your check might read "Custodian X f/b/o (for benefit of) John Doe IRA."

3. **KEEP TRACK OF WHEN YOU RECEIVE YOUR DISTRIBUTION.** Few people know when the 60-day clock actually begins. It starts when you receive the distribution. The few days between when the check was issued and when you actually received it may make all the difference in the world.

4. **CHECK TO MAKE SURE THE FUNDS WERE DEPOSITED INTO THE CORRECT ACCOUNT.** A common mistake occurs when funds are accidentally deposited into a non-retirement account. Once you've deposited the funds or sent them to your financial institution, take five minutes out of your day to make sure they have arrived at their intended destination. If the mistake is discovered within 60 days it can be corrected.

5. **BE AWARE OF THE ONCE-PER-YEAR IRA ROLLOVER RULE.** You are limited in the number of 60-day rollovers you can make in a 365-day period. The once-per-year rollover rule applies only to 60-day rollovers from IRA to IRA or from Roth IRA to Roth IRA. Under the rule, once funds have been rolled over as a 60-day rollover, no other 60-day rollovers can be done by the account owner within the next 365 days. For this rule, IRAs and Roth IRAs are counted together.

PLANNING FOR
MULTIPLE BENEFICIARIES

When do multiple beneficiaries exist?
Multiple beneficiaries exist when an individual names more than one beneficiary for their IRA.

When should you name more than one beneficiary?
When you want your IRA assets to go to more than one person or entity without having to incur additional fees or paperwork by maintaining separate accounts for each beneficiary.

1. DUE DATE FOR DESIGNATED BENEFICIARIES. September 30 of the year following the year of the IRA owner's death is the date designated beneficiaries are determined for purposes of post-death stretch payments.

2. DUE DATE FOR NON-DESIGNATED BENEFICIARIES. These beneficiaries should be cashed-out before the September 30 date mentioned above. These beneficiaries include charities, estates and non-qualifying trusts since they have no measurable life expectancies. If they are not cashed out in time, they could prevent other beneficiaries from being able to stretch out distributions.

3. DUE DATE FOR SEPARATE INHERITED IRAS. These should be established and funded for each designated beneficiary by December 31 of the year following the year of the account owner's death. These accounts must retain the decedent's name as part of their title and include language identifying them as "inherited" or "beneficiary" accounts, but they must use the beneficiary's social security number for reporting purposes.

4. **MAXIMIZE THE STRETCH.** Each designated beneficiary identified by September 30 can utilize his or her own single life expectancy to maximize the stretch IRA if a separate account is established and funded by December 31. The single life expectancy factor is determined in the year following the year of the account owner's death. Going forward, the factor is simply reduced by one each year (unless the sole beneficiary is the spouse, in which case he/she re-determines his/her life expectancy each year).

5. **WHAT IF YOU DON'T SPLIT THE ACCOUNT IN TIME?** The single life expectancy of the oldest beneficiary must be used to calculate payments to all beneficiaries if separate inherited accounts are not established in time.

Avoiding Spousal Beneficiary Mistakes

Who is a spouse beneficiary?

A spouse beneficiary must be married to the account owner at the time of the account owner's death, and he or she must be named on the beneficiary form (or inherit directly through the document default provisions). A spouse beneficiary has a number of unique options.

1. SPLIT THE INHERITED ACCOUNT IF NECESSARY. A spouse beneficiary can take advantage of the special spousal rules if they are the sole beneficiary of an IRA account. If other beneficiaries have been named, the spouse can still take advantage of these special provisions by transferring their portion of the inherited IRA to a separate account by December 31 of the year following the year of the IRA owner's death.

2. WILL A SPOUSE BENEFICIARY NEED MONEY PRIOR TO 59 .? If a spouse beneficiary needs money from the IRA prior to age 59 ., they will likely want to remain a beneficiary of the inherited account. Death is an exception to the 10% early distribution penalty, so by staying as a beneficiary they'll avoid paying the 10% penalty. The account should be retitled as a properly titled inherited IRA. A spouse that remains a beneficiary does not need to take RMDs from the account until the year the deceased spouse would have turned 70 .

3. TRANSFER THE INHERITED IRA INTO A SPOUSE BENEFICIARY'S ACCOUNT. A spouse beneficiary should generally roll the inherited IRA into their own name. Once a younger spouse beneficiary reaches age 59 ., there's no advantage to remaining a beneficiary, and a spouse rollover or transfer should be done. There is no deadline for this transaction. NO other beneficiary has this option. By doing this rollover or transfer, a surviving spouse ensures that their own beneficiaries will be able to stretch distributions over their own life expectancies.

4. **NAME NEW BENEFICIARIES.** A surviving spouse should name their own beneficiaries. If no beneficiaries have been named and the surviving spouse dies, the remaining assets will pass according to the default provisions in the custodial document. This is frequently the estate of the now deceased spouse, which could eliminate the stretch option for beneficiaries or add unnecessary time and expenses by tying the assets up in probate.

5. **CONSIDER A DISCLAIMER.** Before taking any action regarding an inherited IRA, a surviving spouse should evaluate whether a full or partial disclaimer would be advantageous. Using a disclaimer, some or all of the inherited IRA can be passed to contingent beneficiaries, potentially extending the stretch IRA and reducing the future impact of estate taxes.

TO CONVERT OR NOT TO CONVERT

What is a Roth IRA conversion?

A Roth IRA conversion is the process of moving IRA or employer plan assets to a Roth IRA.

1. WHEN WILL YOU NEED THE MONEY? If you have an immediate need for the funds or need them to continue your current standard of living, then a Roth IRA conversion is probably not for you. However, if you have no immediate need for the funds, a Roth IRA conversion is potentially a great way for the funds to grow tax-free over your lifetime.

2. WHERE WILL THE MONEY COME FROM TO PAY THE TAX? In nearly all cases, the money to pay the tax on a Roth IRA conversion should come from outside (non-retirement account) funds in order for the conversion to make sense. When a Roth IRA conversion is made, it generally triggers a taxable event, so your ability to pay that tax with outside money will go a long way in determining whether a Roth IRA conversion is right for you.

3. WHAT DO YOU THINK FUTURE TAX RATES WILL BE? If you believe your income tax rate will be the same or higher in retirement, then converting funds to a Roth IRA NOW makes more sense, since you will be paying the tax at a lower rate. On the other hand, if you think your income tax rate will be much lower in retirement, you may want to forgo a Roth IRA conversion and take advantage of lower tax rates in a later year.

4. **OTHER REASONS TO CONSIDER A ROTH IRA CONVERSION.** You may have favorable tax attributes in the year of the conversion such as large charitable deductions, net operating losses and tax credits; you will not have to take required minimum distributions starting at age 70 .; you will have the ability to make contributions even after age 70 . if there is eligible earned income; you can provide an income-tax-free inheritance to your heirs.

5. **OTHER REASONS TO NOT CONSIDER A ROTH IRA CONVERSION.** You have an aversion to paying the income tax up front; you do NOT trust that the government will keep their tax-free deal; you plan to name a charity as your Roth IRA beneficiary, and it will NOT have to pay income taxes on the money it receives.

RE-CHARACTERIZING
A ROTH CONVERSION

What is a Roth IRA re-characterization?

In the simplest of terms, a Roth IRA re-characterization is an "undo." It erases a Roth IRA conversion, and the conversion is treated as if it never occurred.

1. **MEET THE DEADLINE.** A Roth IRA conversion can be re-characterized until October 15 of the year after the calendar year of conversion. That means that either a January 1, 2014 or a December 31, 2014 conversion can be re-characterized through October 15, 2015. If you miss the October 15 deadline, the only way to get an extension is to go for a private letter ruling from the IRS.

2. **MAKE A TRUSTEE-TO-TRUSTEE TRANSFER BACK TO AN IRA.** A re-characterization must be made via a trustee-to-trustee transfer. Additionally, regardless of where the funds originally came from, all re-characterizations of a Roth IRA conversion must go to a traditional IRA.

3. **KNOW THE DIFFERENCE BETWEEN THE AMOUNT RE-CHARACTERIZED AND THE TOTAL FUNDS TRANSFERRED BACK TO AN IRA.** The re-characterized amount is the total dollar amount (NOT the number of shares) of the initial conversion you wish to undo. But, total funds transferred back must include the earnings (or losses) attributed to the re-characterized amount. Knowing the difference between these two values will help make sure that the re-characterization is properly reported on the tax return.

4. **FIND OUT YOUR ROTH IRA CUSTODIAN'S POLICIES.** Under the Tax Code, you are allowed to re-characterize all or just a portion of a Roth IRA conversion. Your Roth IRA custodian, however, may not be as flexible. This is particularly common with annuities or other contractual investments. In other cases, you may be restricted by account minimums that must be maintained.

5. **GET YOUR MONEY BACK!** If you re-characterize after you have filed your tax return(s) for the year of conversion, you will need to file an amended return(s) so the IRS, and your state, know that you are no longer responsible for tax on the conversion. If you've already paid all or a portion of the tax, you'll get those amounts back... plus interest!

DETERMINING TAX ON ROTH IRA DISTRIBUTIONS

What are the ordering rules?

Roth IRA distributions can consist of contributions, converted funds and earnings – or any combination of the three. To determine what your distribution is, you must use "ordering rules" which dictate the order in which these categories of Roth IRA money must be withdrawn. All Roth IRAs are considered one Roth IRA for distribution purposes. A Roth IRA distribution will consist first of any Roth IRA contributions. If there are no contributions or those amounts are completely exhausted, the next funds out are converted funds. Once all converted funds have been exhausted, the remainder of the distributions will consist of earnings.

1. **ARE YOU WITHDRAWING A CONTRIBUTION?** Roth IRA contributions are the annual amounts that you contribute to a Roth IRA account. A distribution of Roth IRA contributions will always be both tax and penalty free.

2. **ARE YOU WITHDRAWING CONVERTED AMOUNTS BEFORE AGE 59?** Converted funds are never subject to income tax. However, they will be subject to the 10% penalty for early distributions (unless an exception applies) if you are under 59 . and they have been in a Roth IRA for less than five years. Each conversion starts its own 10% PENALTY 5-year clock, and the converted amounts are withdrawn on a first-in, first-out basis.

3. **ARE YOU WITHDRAWING CONVERTED AMOUNTS AFTER 5 YEARS OR AGE 59?** A distribution of converted funds after 5 years or after age 59 . will be entirely income tax and penalty free.

4. **ARE YOU WITHDRAWING EARNINGS BEFORE AGE 59?** Earnings withdrawn prior to age 59 . are generally subject to income tax regardless of how long they've been in a Roth IRA account. Earnings withdrawn prior to age 59 . are also generally subject to the 10% penalty for early distributions unless an exception applies.

5. **ARE YOU WITHDRAWING EARNINGS AFTER AGE 59 AND 5 YEARS?** Earnings withdrawn after age 59 . are never subject to the 10% penalty. They may, however, be subject to income tax. If you have held a Roth IRA for more than 5 years, your earnings are tax free, if not, they are taxable at ordinary rates.

CALCULATING NUA

What is NUA?

NUA is short for "Net Unrealized Appreciation" of employer securities. It's the difference between the cost basis and the market value of employer securities held inside a qualified plan such as a 401(k). To take advantage of a special tax break for NUA, there must be a triggering event [separation from service (unless self-employed), disability (only if self-employed), attainment of age 59 . or death].

When should you consider using NUA?

You should consider using NUA when the cost basis of employer securities in your plan is much lower than the current market value. The special tax break for NUA allows you to pay long-term capital gains rates on the growth of your shares while inside the plan instead of ordinary rates, and you will not owe that tax until the shares are sold outside the plan. This can create up to a 20% tax savings.

1. **FIRST THINGS FIRST.** Look for employer securities and their cost basis on your plan statement. See if the cost basis is higher or lower than the market value. If it is lower, consider NUA.

2. **BE DIRECT WITH YOUR ROLLOVER.** Do a direct rollover of the assets that you want to remain tax-deferred to an IRA or other qualified plan. This will avoid any mandatory withholding and eliminate the possibility of 60-day rollover mistakes.

3. **KINDLY TRANSFER IN-KIND.** Next, transfer the shares of employer securities in-kind (as stock) to a taxable (non-retirement plan) account (this is not a rollover). Do not sell the shares while they are still in your plan. When the employer securities are transferred in-kind to a taxable account, ordinary income tax is owed on the basis of the shares.

4. **THE EARLY BIRD GETS A LUMP-SUM DISTRIBUTION.** In order to qualify for the special NUA tax break, you must make a "lump-sum distribution" where the entire plan balance is distributed in one calendar year. Start the distribution early in the calendar year to ensure it is completed in time.

5. **RMD PERK.** The cost basis of the employer securities in the NUA distribution can be used to satisfy your required minimum distribution (RMD) for the year of distribution (if you have one).

CALCULATING THE PRO-RATA RULE

What is the pro-rata rule?

The pro-rata rule is the formula used to determine how much of a distribution is taxable when the account owner holds both after-tax and pre-tax dollars in their IRA(s). For the purposes of the pro-rata rule, the IRS looks at all your SEP, SIMPLE, and Traditional IRAs as if they were one. Even if you have been making after-tax contributions to a separate account for years, and there have been no earnings, you cannot isolate your after-tax amounts and must take your other IRAs into consideration.

1. **TOTAL UP ALL OF YOUR IRAS.** Calculate the total balance of all of your IRAs. Include the balances from each of your IRA accounts, including SEP IRAs and SIMPLE IRAs. Roth IRA balances and balances from any non-IRA based company plans are NOT included for this purpose.

2. **TOTAL UP ALL AFTER-TAX DOLLARS IN IRAS.** Calculate the total balance of all after-tax dollars in all of your IRAs. After-tax dollars are either non-deductible contributions made directly to an IRA or rollovers of after-tax dollars from a company plan. If this is not the first year you have had after-tax dollars in your IRA, you should be able to find the previous year's after-tax total on IRS Form 8606.

3. **CALCULATE YOUR PERCENTAGE OF AFTER-TAX DOLLARS.** Divide your after-tax IRA dollars (step 2) by your total IRA balance (step 1). If you have $20,000 of after-tax dollars in all your IRAs and the total balance of all your IRAs is $100,000, your percentage of after-tax dollars is 20% ($20,000/$100,000 = 20%).

4. **DETERMINE THE TAXABLE AMOUNT OF YOUR DISTRIBUTION.** Take the total of all your distribution and multiply it by the percentage you have arrived at in step #3. This is the total amount of the distribution that is tax free. If, in our example, a distribution of $10,000 was made, the tax-free portion would be $2,000 (20% x $10,000 = $2,000). The remaining portion of the distribution ($8,000) would be taxable at ordinary rates.

5. **EXCEPTION FOR ROLLOVERS TO A COMPANY PLAN OR CHARITABLE ROLLOVERS.** Under the Tax Code, only pre-tax dollars can be rolled from an IRA into a company plan. If you are making a rollover from your IRA to a company plan, disregard the pro-rata rule altogether. Just be careful not to roll over more than the total amount of pre-tax dollars in your IRA. Qualified charitable distributions (QCDs) from IRAs also disregard the pro-rata rule.

Using a Tax Refund
to Fund an IRA

What does the basic process entail?

An income tax refund can be directly deposited to an IRA up to the annual contribution limit. The contribution limit is $5,500 ($6,500 for individuals age 50 or older) for 2014 and 2015. It can also be split among multiple accounts.

1. **IT IS TAX TIME!** Prepare your tax return for the year.

2. **DETERMINE THE REFUND AMOUNT.** Once you know how big your refund will be, decide how much, if any, you would like to contribute to your IRA or Roth IRA up to the maximum annual contribution allowed.

3. **ONE, TWO, THREE.** A refund going to only one account can be done directly on IRS Form 1040. Prepare IRS Form 8888 to direct the refund to up to three accounts.

4. **WATCH OUT!** If you use Form 8888, pay attention to the six cautions provided by the IRS on the instructions to ensure that you do not fall into any of those traps. The form can be found on the IRS' website (www.irs.gov).

5. **FOLLOW-UP, FOLLOW-UP, FOLLOW-UP.** If the IRA deposit is meant to be for the prior year, make sure the institution will code it that way, and that it is received in time. If the refund amount is adjusted for math errors or tax adjustments, check which accounts on the form are affected. You may need to do an amended return if the IRA deposit is adjusted. Refund offsets can be done against any accounts receiving the refund. Again, you may need to do an amended return. If the funds go into the wrong account, deal with the institution to get the funds credited to the correct account.

Navigating the Health Care Taxes

What is considered investment income?

In 2010, the health care laws created 3.8% surtax on net investment income starting in 2013. Below is a list of what is and is not considered investment income.

Investment Income: Interest, dividends, capital gains (long and short), annuities (not those in IRAs or company plans), royalty income, passive rental income, other passive activity income
NOT Investment Income: Wages and self-employment income, active trade/business income, distributions from IRAs, Roth IRAs, employer plans, excluded gain from sale of a principal residence, municipal bond interest, proceeds of life insurance policies, veterans' benefits, Social Security benefits, gains on sale of an active interest in a partnership or S corporation

1. IDENTIFY THE SURTAX INCOME THRESHOLDS. The first step is to know the MAGI (modified adjusted gross income) thresholds to avoid the 3.8% surtax on net investment income. They are as follows: Married Filing Jointly ($250,000); Individuals ($200,000); Married Filing Separately ($125,000); Trusts and Estates ($12,400 for 2016). Trusts and estates are hit particularly hard with the surtax kicking in at a much lower income level.

2. LOOK AT TAXABLE INCOME. Taxable income from all sources can push taxpayers over the MAGI threshold and cause their investment income to be subject to the 3.8% surtax. Income tax-free Roth distributions will NOT affect MAGI.

3. **UNDERSTAND HOW MUCH WILL BE TAXED.** The 3.8% surtax is imposed on the lesser of (1) net investment income or (2) the amount of MAGI over the certain income threshold. Taxpayers with income below those MAGI levels will NOT be subject to this tax.

4. **KNOW OTHER HEALTH CARE TAX PROVISIONS EFFECTIVE SINCE 2013.** The 3.8% surtax gets the attention, but there is also an additional 0.9% Medicare tax on wages and self-employment income over the MAGI thresholds. Also, medical expenses must exceed 10% of AGI (up from 7.5%) to be deductible (if age 65 or older, this provision is effective in 2017). That 10% also applies to the medical expense exception to the 10% penalty on early IRA or plan withdrawals.

5. **DISCUSS THESE TAX PLANNING POINTS.** You need to know that while IRA and plan distributions are exempt from the surtax, taxable distributions from these accounts can push income over MAGI thresholds. Roth conversions can be a valuable tool to eliminate future taxable income, especially for taxpayers with significant investment income or a discretionary trust as their IRA beneficiary. However, conversions could push you above your threshold in the short-term. Salary deferrals (401(k)s for example) can reduce MAGI for the 3.8% surtax but NOT for the 0.9% additional Medicare tax.

Protecting an IRA from Prohibited Transactions

What is a prohibited transaction?
A prohibited transaction occurs when an IRA owner uses IRA assets in a self-serving or self-dealing manner that improperly benefits the IRA owner.

When should you look for a prohibited transaction?
It may be a prohibited transaction anytime an IRA owner or beneficiary has a self-directed IRA account invested in a business in which the account owner also engages outside of the IRA, has unexplained large deposits or balances in the IRA, or funnels business expenses or income through a Roth IRA.

1. **WHO DOES IT BENEFIT?** Make sure that all IRA transactions are done for the benefit of the IRA only. All transactions should be arms length transactions and should be made at current market rates.

2. **PERSONAL AND IRA ASSETS DON'T MESH.** Do not co-mingle personal assets and IRA assets or use personal assets for the benefit of the IRA or its assets. For example, if your IRA owns a rental home, you cannot spend time at the rental home, even if you pay your IRA the fair market rent that any other third party would.

3. **YOU CAN'T MAKE A DEAL WITH YOUR IRA.** You cannot borrow from your IRA, lend to your IRA, or pledge your IRA assets as collateral for a loan.

4. **WATCH OUT FOR PROMOTIONAL SCAMS.** Promoters/ promotions that say a strategy is approved by the IRS are trying to pull a fast one. IRS does NOT approve or recommend IRA transactions or investments.

5. **TOO MANY COOKS IN THE KITCHEN.** A transaction that requires multiple entities to accomplish a strategy that would not normally be allowed in an IRA is probably a prohibited transaction.

AVOIDING 72(T) MISTAKES

What are 72(t) payments?

72(t) payments are a series of substantially equal periodic payments made from an IRA that can be used to avoid the 10% penalty for early distributions. Payments must last the greater of 5 years or until the IRA owner reaches age 59 . When using a 72(t) schedule, a number of changes are prohibited. If these changes occur, the 10% penalty (and interest) is applied retroactively to all distributions made prior to age 59 .

1. **SEPARATE YOUR ACCOUNTS FIRST.** When you establish a 72(t) payment plan, the distributions can be calculated using the balance(s) of one or more IRA accounts. But once the 72(t) schedule is in place, the rules significantly restrict your ability to make changes to the accounts without incurring penalties. So, split your IRA account(s) before you set up the plan. Leave only the minimum amount needed to produce your desired payment in accounts used to calculate the distributions.

2. **MAKE SURE TO WAIT A FULL 5 YEARS.** 72(t) payments must be maintained for at least 5 full years after the date of the first distribution. If you are taking distributions annually, this DOES NOT mean that after your fifth distribution, you're done. You must wait until the end of the fifth year before making any transactions that would result in a modification.

3. **DO NOT ADD TO OR SUBTRACT FROM ACCOUNTS.** Other than by the 72(t) distributions themselves, once a 72(t) payment plan is established, the account balance can only be changed by the earnings and losses within the account. NO additional contributions (including any rollovers or direct transfers) into the account may be made, and NO additional distributions can be taken.

4. **TRY TO AVOID THEM.** The 72(t) distribution rules are extremely restrictive and in most cases should only be used as a last resort. Before setting up these plans, be sure you've exhausted all of your other options. You may want to consider a home equity loan or check to see if your 401(k) or other plan offers a loan feature.

5. **NO ROLLOVERS OR CONVERSIONS OF PAYMENTS.** Sometimes financial circumstances change after the 72(t) payment schedule has been set up and the distributions are no longer needed. 72(t) payments cannot be rolled over into another (or the same) IRA and they cannot be converted to a Roth IRA. Instead, consider using the funds to start a "rainy day fund" in a non-retirement account in case another financial hardship occurs.

AVOIDING MISTAKES IN A DIVORCE

Retirement accounts and divorce

When a divorce occurs, the financial assets of a couple, including their retirement accounts, are often split. If mistakes are made during this process, the stress of a divorce can be compounded when one or both spouses find that they are subject to unnecessary taxes or penalties.

1. IRAS IN DIVORCE. To properly divide an IRA as a result of a divorce, specific language on the structure of "who gets what" should be included in the marital settlement agreement (MSA) or other divorce agreement. A copy of this executed agreement should be given to the IRA custodian. The money should NOT simply be withdrawn from the IRA and given to the other spouse, as this would be treated as a taxable distribution for the IRA owner. The funds should instead be transferred to the receiving spouse's IRA.

2. QUALIFIED PLANS IN DIVORCE. Qualified plans can't be split by an MSA or divorce agreement. They require a special court order, known as a Qualified Domestic Relations Order (QDRO). Once a QDRO has been issued, it should be sent to the qualified plan's administrator. The terms of the plan will determine when the spouse receives the funds. In some plans, a lump-sum distribution will be available immediately, while in other plans, benefits may not be payable until the ex-spouse retires.

3. **WHAT TO DO WITH THE RECEIVED FUNDS.** If you are receiving a portion of an IRA, you will likely want to move the funds over to your own IRA to avoid incurring tax and possibly the 10% early distribution penalty. However, If you are receiving a distribution pursuant to a QDRO, you will want to consider if you will be using any of the funds prior to age 59 . Funds received directly from a plan under a QDRO are exempt from the 10% penalty. If you roll those funds over to an IRA and later take a distribution prior to age 59 ., the 10% early distribution penalty will apply.

4. **NAME NEW/UPDATE BENEFICIARIES.** One of the most common mistakes after a divorce is the failure to properly update beneficiary forms. This is NOT something that should be overlooked. There have been many documented cases where a failure to properly update beneficiary forms led to an ex-spouse receiving funds that were intended for children or even a new spouse. DON'T let this happen to you.

5. **REASSESS RETIREMENT PREPAREDNESS.** For many, a divorce is an emotionally draining and traumatic event. But for some, the emotional impact is compounded by a significant change to personal finances. So just like any other major life event, it's beneficial to reevaluate your retirement and financial plans to determine the best course of action.

Avoiding Charitable IRA Beneficiary Mistakes

Can IRAs be used to benefit a charity?

IRAs can be a great source of funds to provide a benefit for a favorite charity, but using these funds can create a number of traps that must be avoided in order to maximize benefits to both the charity and other IRA beneficiaries.

1. **NAME THE CHARITY DIRECTLY ON YOUR BENEFICIARY FORM.** The money will go directly to the charity, avoiding both the time and expense of probate. Additionally, the distribution to the charity will not be considered income to the estate of the deceased IRA owner.

2. **SET UP SEPARATE ACCOUNTS.** Consider transferring the portion you intend to leave to charity into a separate IRA account. If other beneficiaries inherit the same IRA as a charity and the charity's portion is not "cashed out" or split within the IRS prescribed time frames, the stretch IRA for the living beneficiaries will be lost.

3. **REVERSE YOUR BEQUESTS.** If you have made provisions for certain charities under your will and also have retirement plans, an effective tax strategy would be to reverse the bequests with non-retirement assets. This way, the charity receives the same amount that you were going to leave them in your will, but your heirs will end up with more, because the money they will inherit will not be subject to income tax, as the retirement plan would be.

4. **DON'T CONVERT ASSETS YOU PLAN TO LEAVE TO A CHARITY.** Many charitable organizations and religious groups are structured tax-exempt organizations. When an IRA is left to one of these charities, the charity does not have to pay income tax on the distribution as other beneficiaries would. As a result, if you intend to leave your IRA to charity, converting it to a Roth IRA is generally not a wise move. Why pay income tax on the conversion when the money will be going to the charity tax free anyway?

5. **BEWARE OF NAMING A CHARITY AS A TRUST BENEFICIARY.** A charity is known as a "non designated beneficiary," because it does not have a life expectancy. In general, trusts are also non-designated beneficiaries. Certain trusts, known as see-through (or look-through) trusts allow for post-death distributions to be stretched based on the trust beneficiary with the shortest remaining life expectancy. Since a charity has no life expectancy, if it is named as a beneficiary of a trust that is also inheriting an IRA, it can eliminate the stretch for the remaining trust beneficiaries.

Planning for a Disclaimer

What is a disclaimer?

A disclaimer is a formal refusal of an inheritance (or part of an inheritance) by a beneficiary. By creating a "path" for disclaimed assets to follow, a skilled planner can provide a beneficiary with the option to pass assets to alternate beneficiaries.

1. **MAKE SURE THE IRA OWNER NAMES CONTINGENT BENEFICIARIES.** Naming a contingent beneficiary directly on the beneficiary form is good practice and a pivotal part of most disclaimer planning. When a disclaimer is executed, the person making the disclaimer is treated as if he or she had predeceased the IRA owner. The contingent beneficiary would then inherit the property. If there is no contingent beneficiary listed, often times the funds will default to the estate of the deceased IRA owner.

2. **TOUCH NOTHING AFTER DEATH! IN ORDER TO EXECUTE A DISCLAIMER, BENEFICIARIES CANNOT HAVE "ACCEPTED" THE PROPERTY.** Typically, this includes taking distributions from the account, actively transferring the account or making investment changes within the account. An exception does exist, however, for a beneficiary taking the year of death required minimum distribution for a deceased account owner.

3. **CONSULT WITH A QUALIFIED ESTATE PLANNING ATTORNEY.** A disclaimer isn't a simple form you get from your IRA custodian that you just sign and send back. It's a legal document generally prepared by an estate planning attorney. Since property law is governed primarily at the state level, there may be slight variations from state to state regarding how the disclaimer must actually be executed or worded.

4. **BE MINDFUL OF THE DEADLINE.** Under the Tax Code, a disclaimer must be delivered to the IRA custodian, in writing, within nine months of the date of the IRA owner's death. In the case of a beneficiary who inherits prior to age 21, the disclaimer must be made within nine months of turning 21.

5. **REVIEW THE DISCLAIMER'S IMPACT.** There is no changing course with a disclaimer. Once it's been executed, you can't go back. Before you disclaim, make sure you've considered all implications. Will it trigger an estate or generation skipping tax? Will it leave a beneficiary with too little? Will it give another beneficiary too much?

CALCULATING AN IRD DEDUCTION

What is an IRD (Income in Respect of a Decedent) deduction?
An IRD deduction is a way of offsetting the impact of double taxation (federal estate tax and income tax) on certain inherited assets. It's an income tax deduction for the beneficiary (miscellaneous itemized deduction, not subject to limitations).

When should you look for an IRD deduction?
When an individual receives a 1099-R for a distribution that has code 4 (the death code) in Box 7. Don't expect the CPA to pick up on this. In the tax time crunch it is easily overlooked.

1. **FIND OUT THE AMOUNT OF FEDERAL ESTATE TAX PAID BY THE DECEDENT.** It's listed on page 1 of the decedent's estate tax return, Form 706.

2. **CREATE AN IMAGINARY ESTATE TAX RETURN THAT ASSUMES NO IRA.** You'll need an estate tax planning software program to do it. Plug in the value of the estate after subtracting the value of the IRA. This will tell you what the federal estate tax would have been if there were no IRA in the estate.

3. **SUBTRACTION.** Subtract the imaginary federal estate tax as if there were no IRA (figured in step 2) from the federal estate actually paid (in step 1). That result is the amount of the IRD deduction.

4. **DIVISION.** Divide the IRD deduction (from step 3) by the amount of the IRA included in the estate. This will give you the percentage of the deduction you (the beneficiary) will be able to claim at each withdrawal from the inherited IRA.

5. **MULTIPLICATION.** Multiply the amount of the IRA distribution you took during the year by the percentage in step 4 to get the amount of your annual IRD deduction. You cannot claim this deduction in a year that you did not withdraw from the inherited IRA.

Examining Qualifying Longevity Annuity Contracts

What is a QLAC (Qualifying Longevity Annuity Contract)?
A QLAC is a type of fixed income annuity that has special attributes and is held in a retirement account.

1. **RMD (REQUIRED MINIMUM DISTRIBUTION) EXCLUSION.** The fair market value of your QLAC is excluded from your RMD calculations. What's the benefit? You can keep a greater portion of your IRA (or other retirement account) intact longer while enhancing the income stream the annuity will provide in the future.

2. **THE DISTRIBUTION DEADLINE.** You don't have to start taking distributions from your QLACs at age 70 1/2, but you can't delay them indefinitely. QLAC distributions must begin no later than the first day of the month after you turn age 85.

3. **YOUR INVESTMENT THRESHOLD.** You will be limited as to how much of your retirement savings you can invest in a QLAC. The limit will be the lesser of $125,000 or 25% of your applicable retirement account assets. The 25% limit applies on a per account basis except for IRAs, BUT the $125,000 is a cumulative limit for all QLACs in all retirement accounts. For IRAs, the 25% limit will apply to the prior year-end total of all IRAs (not including Roth IRAs).

4. **FACTS TO KEEP IN MIND.** QLACs cannot be variable or equity-indexed annuity contracts, though insurance companies may offer contracts with cost-of-living adjustments. QLACs cannot offer any cash surrender value. So if you buy one, just be sure you won't be needing that lump-sum of money anytime soon!

5. **THE DEATH BENEFIT.** QLACs can offer two death benefit options: a life annuity (the rules can vary depending on a number of factors) and a return-of-premium option. These, of course, are the potential death benefit options allowed by the tax code, but that doesn't mean that every QLAC contract will offer all of these options.